House Flipping
– Beginners Guide

The Ultimate Fix and Flip Strategies on How to Find, Buy, Fix, and Then Sell at a Profit to Achieve Financial Freedom from Real Estate Investing

David Hewitt & Andrew Peter

By reading this document, the reader agrees that under no circumstances is the author responsible for any losses, direct or indirect, that are incurred as a result of the use of the information contained within this document, including, but not limited to, errors, omissions, or inaccuracies.

Table of Contents

Introduction

Chapter One: First Concepts

Chapter Two: Preparing Your Financing

Chapter Three: Find Your Agent (s)

Chapter Four: Where You Should Buy

Chapter Five: What You Should Buy

Chapter Six: Who to Buy From

Chapter Seven: How You'll Find Deals

Chapter Eight: The Flip Formula

Chapter Nine: Looking at Properties

Chapter Ten: Making Offers

Chapter Eleven: Your Due Diligence

Chapter Twelve: Create Your SOW

Chapter Thirteen: Create Your Budget

Chapter Fourteen: Create Your Schedule

Chapter Fifteen: Hiring Contractors

Chapter Sixteen: Managing Your Rehab

Chapter Seventeen: Agent or FSBO?

Chapter Eighteen: Staging

Chapter Nineteen: Buyer Due Diligence

Chapter Twenty: The Closing

Final Words

Introduction

House flipping programs on HGTV and other cable networks have inspired a keen interest in real estate investment. The good news is that real estate investing still remains one of the best ways to create wealth and build residual income over time. However, there is still a science to it. It's not like you can jump in and buy a house, paint a few walls, and then expect to flip that home for profit. There is research involved. You need to know the market, how to negotiate, how to build a budget, and close on a sale, just to name a few things. This book is designed to guide you through the process of house flipping, from preparing your financing options to the close.

The high demand of the market creates the perfect opportunity for a new real estate investor to purchase and sell houses quickly, increasing the profit margin. In some hot markets across the country, homes can sell in 3-7 days. Chief economist for the National Association of Realtors, Lawrence Yun, predicted that new home sales will increase by 21% in 2021, increasing wealth of homeowners (Orton, 2021). This presents an incredible opportunity for existing and potential estate investors, which is one of the reasons I wrote this book.

This book is designed to walk you through all of the necessary steps to launch a successful career as a house flipper and real estate investor. Given the unpredictability of our market, building assets through real estate can provide you with the financial stability you need to weather the storm. We will walk you through the basic concepts of house flipping in case this is a concept that is completely new to you. From there, we will show you all of the steps necessary to procure your first property, from securing your financing to working with realtors and other industry experts. What you will learn early in this process is there is a lot of research involved. We understand that it's not a very sexy part of the job, but without it, you won't have a flip, so please take the steps in the process seriously. After you've done your research, you can start searching for the right property. We will educate you on the different types of properties and where you should buy as a new investor. After you've found your first property, you're going to run some numbers to see if this property is the best option for you. That's where we'll introduce the flip formula to guide your math. After you've chosen your property and made your offer—which we'll walk you through as well—you can build your scope of work, which will be the first steps to outlining your budget and schedule. We cover all of this and more in this guidebook.

If you are willing to put in the necessary sweat equity and follow the steps in this book, you will be on your way to creating wealth as a house flipper. Now is the perfect time to grab your real estate market share. Time is of the essence, as you never know how long markets stay hot for or when they cool down. If you want to ride the rising real estate wave that is cresting, the time is now to learn.

In this book, we will outline these twenty steps to launch you into your first rehab:

1. Defining the concept of house flipping.

2. Preparing your financing.

3. Finding an agent to work with.

4. Determining where you should buy.

5. What kind of property should you buy?

6. Who to buy from.

7. How to find deals.

8. Your flip formula.

9. Looking at properties.

10. Making offers.

11. Your due diligence.

12. Creating your SOW.

13. Creating your budget.

14. Creating your schedule.

15. Hiring contractors.

16. Managing your rehab.

17. Using an agent or For Sale By Owner.

18. Staging.

19. Buyer due diligence.

20. The closing.

Chapter One: First Concepts

Before you jump into your first house flip, it's important that you understand some of the basic fundamentals of house flipping, starting with the basic definition. Flipping a house simply means that you purchase it with the intent of selling it quickly to earn a profit (How to flip a house, 2020). When the real estate climate is fertile for house flipping, house sales rise. If the market has created an environment where more people want to own an asset, the people will likely take advantage of the lower interest rates to invest in a home. Also during some specific events, people may want to spend more time at home, also creating more of a demand for home sales. It's good to infer people's attitude toward current global and local events. The result? Real estate investing and house flipping is more relevant today than it has ever been.

Can you make a good living as a house flipper? That depends upon your market and how many houses you can flip each year. If you can manage a consistent rehab schedule, which we will discuss later in this book, you can earn a strong income as a house flipper. The general rule of thumb is that you don't want to invest in a property that won't yield you 10-15% in profit after expenses. Anything less than this is costing you money rather than making it. Although the range is variable, experienced flippers usually hope to earn at least $25,000 per flip (Home Shows, How much do house flippers make). As a novice flipper, you can expect to earn a little less than this, but just follow the formula of the 10-15% I mentioned earlier, and you should be just fine.

As a new house flipper, you will be earning your income in lump sums. Therefore, it is important that you are privy to tax rules, as they imply to real estate investing to avoid a potential audit. The IRS does not consider real estate investing to be passive income, but active income. The result? You'll be placed in a higher tax bracket, resulting in 10% - 37%. You'll also be subject to self-employment tax. As you are planning your income, it is imperative that you factor these expenses in (Ivy, 2019).

9

Many new house flippers wonder how viable it is to flip houses part-time. Although you want the financial benefits of house flipping, you don't want to give up a potential steady income if you have a full-time job. Can you flip houses part-time? The short answer to this question is yes. It is a simple way to get started in this business at a low risk. It is important to understand that if you are flipping part-time, your rehabs will typically take longer because you are splitting your time. That means you will not be able to flip as many homes as you would if you were a full-time investor, also meaning that your income potential will be less (Kidd, Is flipping houses part-time or on the side possible). If you are just looking to make a part-time, side hustle income, then this is fine. However, if you would like to build a full-time income from house flipping, you will need to plan a transition to work as an investor full-time to capitalize on your full income potential.

Chapter Summary

- Definition of house flipping.

- Relevancy of house flipping in your market.

- Money you can earn as a house flipper.

- Taxes and house flipping.

- House flipping part-time.

In the next chapter, you will learn how to prepare your financing for your first flip.

Chapter Two: Preparing Your Financing

Now that you understand the basics of house flipping, it's important that you review your finance options when buying your first house.

Hard money loan. You can approach a bank for a traditional loan for your first house. Depending upon interest rates, this may be a viable option for house flippers with a strong credit score.

Friends and family. If you don't want to resort to a loan or lack the collateral or credit score to secure funding, consider approaching your friends and family for fiscal support. If you present this to them as an investment where they will receive a return, you might be surprised at the level of support you will receive. Pitch it as a way for them to earn money, too.

Cash out on existing investments like home equity or 401k. If you have equity in your own home, you could consider a home equity loan to fund your first flip. If you've been at your job for a while, you could also borrow against your 401k to fund your first project.

Partner with another investor. If you know other investors or network with other real estate investors, consider a partnership. If you don't mind splitting the profit, you could work with another investor that could provide funding while you put in the sweat equity. You could even consider taking a lesser percentage to work with a more experienced house flipper, so you can learn more on the job and earn your first lump sum.

Chapter Summary

- Options to secure financing for your first flip.

- Secure a hard money loan.

- Ask friends and family.

- Cash out on investments.

- Partner with another investor.

In the next chapter, you will learn how to secure a real estate agent or become one yourself.

Chapter Three: Find Your Agent(s)

To access the best real estate deals, especially in a market where supply is limited, it is important to find and partner with real estate agents in your market. When searching for a real estate agent to work with, you will want one who is investor-friendly.

An investor-friendly agent is defined as "a licensed real estate professional who has experience with real estate properties, has worked with investors, and has knowledge of the local market. Said agent will be an investor, as well. They will help find deals, analyze them, make offers, and sell properties as necessary" (Shields, Do you need an investor friendly agent to buy an investment property).

If you would like to pocket all of your profit on your real estate deals, you might want to consider becoming a real estate agent yourself. Although getting your license will require some investment in time and education, it can benefit your business in several ways.

- It will provide more visibility to investment opportunities. As an agent, you will have access to the MLS, which will allow you to see homes on the market, sometimes before they are available to the public.

- Becoming an agent opens up another revenue opportunity for you as an investor. You will earn a 6% commission on each house you sell, increasing your investment profit margin. If you're not an agent, you will have to give up this income and factor that into your overall profit on each deal. There may also be other deals available that you may not invest in but sell, enabling you to earn a 6% commission.

- Being your agent gives you more leverage on the entire deal because you are in control of the entire process.

- Agents are required to invest in continuing education to keep your license active. This is beneficial to you as an investor because you will stay up to date on the market and changes as they happen (Real Estate Express, 5 Advantages of Getting a License for Real Estate Investment)

Chapter Summary

- Consider an investor-friendly real estate agent.

- Get your real estate license to create a secondary income and leverage your investment deals.

In the next chapter, you will learn how to farm an area and determine where to buy.

Chapter Four: Where You Should Buy

In real estate, the name of the game is location, location, location. Once you partner with an agent or become one yourself, it is imperative that you find the best locations to buy. It will do you no good to buy a house at $50,000 if all the homes in the neighborhood sell for no more than $60,000. You want to make a profit. There is a science to this process. You want to find neighborhoods and areas that are on the rise, where you can find a home at a great rate, flip it, and sell it for an amazing profit. So how do you find these golden opportunities? How do you know where to buy?

This is where you will have to tap into your left brain analytics. Start the process by reviewing market information for your area. If you are partnered with a real estate agent, they can assist you with this, but you will also want to supplement their work. Of course, if you've chosen to get licensed yourself, you can use resources like the MLS to fuel your research. But the options are vast. Learn about the market around you from the local newspaper, the Census Bureau, and the National Association of Realtors. Learn about the demographics of each market, such as the median income and how homes are selling. Review historical data on the neighborhood and home you are considering. This will provide insight into whether your market is trending up or down. You don't want to buy a home that has been losing value over the years.

Next, you want to research the market status. Is it a rental or a buyer's market? How long are homes staying on the market before they rent or sell? This will provide considerable insight into how your investment will fare, should you choose to flip there. The state of the market will often dictate whether you're in a buyers or sellers market. For example, after the 2008 market crash, the sellers' market decreased, but the renters market was on fire. Since so many people were losing their jobs and foreclosure rates were high, people were afraid to invest in homes. Lenders were not handing out loans, and the market just was not buyer-friendly. You need to watch for current trends in the world and market. During certain trends and happenings in the world, interest rates may fluctuate. That is why it's important to do your research.

Calculate your cash on cash return. "It lets you compare annual cash income against the cash you invested..to calculate your cash on cash return, divide your annual pre-tax cash flow by cash invested" (Moore, The Beginner's Guide to Real Estate Market Analysis).

As you are calculating your cash on return, consider your expenses. If you've done accurate research on your neighborhood, you should be well-informed on what kind of finishes and upgrades to include in your flip. For example, you don't want to invest in granite or quartz in a lower income neighborhood where laminate would do just fine. The goal is to earn a return on your income plus profit. That means you sometimes have to take your personal taste and preference out of it. Be practical and make choices that are going to put money into your pocket and not take it away.

Chapter Summary

- Conduct a market analysis of your area to learn demographics and historical data.

- Are you in a renters or buyers market? Know your market conditions.

- Calculate cash on cash return.

- Evaluate expenses of your flip and match your upgrades with your neighborhood.

In the next chapter, you will learn what kind of properties you should buy.

Chapter Five: What You Should Buy

Once you have learned about the market, it is now time to determine what kind of property you should buy. There are several options to consider. You could buy distressed properties, foreclosed properties, or retail properties. There are pros and cons to each. Let's take a moment to look into each of these options to determine which would be best for you.

Distressed properties. "A distressed property is a property that is on the brink of foreclosure or already owned by the bank" (Johnson, 2020). Though distressed properties provide a way to make higher profit since you can buy them at a discount, it is a tightrope when trying to balance the cost versus the expenses. It is possible that you may find distressed property in a great neighborhood where homes are selling like hotcakes, but the house needs so much work that you don't stand to make a profit. In cases like this, you don't want to become jaded by smoke and mirrors and walk out losing money. For the most part, distressed properties are a great option to consider when flipping a house, but you want to consider some criteria when evaluating this option.

- Know the market value of your neighborhood. One of the best benefits of distressed properties is low cost, but how low? Make sure you stand to make a profit when buying a distressed property. If the highest valued home in the neighborhood is $80,000, then a $70,000 property is not a good buy.

- Be prepared for a large investment. Distressed properties require more TLC. You need to make sure you have the proper investment budget to make the home sellable.

- Be prepared for unexpected risks. Like any flip, you want to have a contingency. Many problems hide beneath the surface of the home like termites, septic issues, and asbestos. Unfortunately, these problems are also the most costly. Be prepared (Clothier, 4 must- knows before taking on a distressed property).

Foreclosed properties. There are some similarities between distressed properties and foreclosed properties, since both are owned by the bank. The good news with foreclosed properties is all foreclosed properties are not necessarily in bad shape, and you can purchase them below market value. You can also secure good financing options on these homes because the banks are eager to unload them. However, like distressed properties, you want to go into these deals with your eyes open and a strategy to ensure you walk away with a profit. When buying foreclosed homes, be prepared for the following:

- High competition. Who doesn't want to buy a house at a discounted rate? The high competition among investors can often lead to a bidding war, which means you may have to spend more money out of pocket than anticipated. The heightened competition can also extend your buying process, which will extend your overall timeline on the project.

- Not always ideal for the novice investor. Although foreclosed properties seem like a great way to get started, it's not an ideal start for a new investor. Dealing with the banks and coming up with the best offers takes time and experience. Foreclosed properties also carry more risk, which a new investor won't be able to afford (Hamed, 2018).

Retail properties. The last option to consider are your retail properties. These opportunities are a bit more cut and dry compared to your distressed and foreclosed properties. There is less risk involved, as these homes usually require less work, but they will often require a higher upfront investment. That simply means you need to brush up on your negotiating skills as a new investor. This is also where partnering up with a real estate agent or becoming one yourself will come in handy. Access to homes through tools like the MLS will reveal deals you would be unable to find otherwise.

Chapter Summary

- Evaluate different options for buying: retail, distressed, foreclosed homes.

- Distressed homes can be bought at a discount but may carry more risk.

- Foreclosed homes are great buys but come with a lot of competition and may not be ideal for novice investors.

- Retail properties provide less risk for a new investor and can partner well with a real estate agent.

In the next chapter, you will learn who to buy your investment property from.

Chapter Six: Who to Buy From

When evaluating who to buy your investment property from, there are two basic categories: bank-owned or private seller. The most important characteristic to consider when evaluating your seller is that you want someone who is motivated.

Private sellers. The majority of homes that you will purchase will be from private sellers. If you are evaluating homes with an agent and using tools like the MLS, you will be able to identify various deals that can fit your specific needs. You may be wondering what exactly qualifies someone as a motivated seller.

- Home has been on the market for an extended period of time. If your seller's home has been sitting on the market for a long time, they are going to be motivated to get rid of it. This will give you leverage to negotiate a lower rate. However, before you jump into a deal, make sure you investigate why the home has been on the market for so long. The answers you find may be the difference between you making a deal or walking away.

- Estate sale. When a family member has passed away and the family is sorting out the details of their estate, they are often motivated to sell so they can move on with their lives.

- Seller has already purchased another home. No one wants to carry a double mortgage. Once your seller has bought another home, they are on a race to sell their old home as quickly as possible to avoid paying two mortgages.

Bank-owned properties. If you opt to purchase distressed or foreclosed properties, you will have to work with a bank. As mentioned previously, this will require a higher level of skill in negotiating, which is not ideal for a new investor. It is recommended that if you purchase a bank-owned property that you work with someone with more experience, such as another investor or real estate agent.

Chapter Summary

- Buy your first home from a private owner or the bank.

- You want to buy from a motivated seller

- Consider partnering up with an experienced investor or agent on bank-owned properties.

In the next chapter, you will learn how to find deals.

Chapter Seven: How You'll Find Deals

Now that you know the types of properties that exist in the marketplace, it is time to find your own deals. Being a successful investor hinges upon utilizing the resources available to you. One of the first things you want to do is identify your niche so you can develop a strategy. Know what type of property you are going after, whether it is retail, foreclosed, or distressed. Know the area you want to focus and how you want to plan to approach it.

Once you've identified your foundation, you will want to start your search. There are a number of ways to find your deals. Try several and stick with the ones that work the best for you.

Networking. Between online marketplaces and local area groups, you can uncover good deals by networking with other professionals in the industry. It will also help you find allies that will work with you long-term on finding deals, so this experience is invaluable. If you're an introvert, we're sorry, but it's time to get out of your comfort zone.

Maximize the MLS. You should have access to the MLS, whether it is through a real estate agent you're partnered with or you've chosen to become a license agent yourself. Some flags to look for when reviewing these listings include: homes that have been on the listing for an extended period of time, homes that were removed and relisted, and expired listings. These are going to be opportunities where the seller is motivated and ready to strike a deal with you.

Partner with wholesalers. Wholesalers are motivated to help you find the motivated sellers you need. You will have to share your profit or provide a finding fee when working with them, but they will bring you opportunities you would otherwise not find.

Mortgage brokers and title companies. These guys are in the know about who is actively selling and buying. Building an alliance with them will allow you to uncover more off-market deals.

Grassroots driving for dollars. There's no better way to uncover opportunities than just driving around your neighborhoods to see what is for sale. There is more to this process than just driving by. Put your interviewing skills to the test and talk to neighbors in the area. Learn more about the neighborhood and opportunities that might come available.

Advertising. Post signs around your neighborhood. Invest in a direct mail campaign and consider online ads to drive leads for deals (Rohde, 2021).

Chapter Summary

- Identify your niche and build a strategy.

- Network to find off-market deals.

- Utilize the MLS.

- Drive for a dollar.

- Invest in advertising.

In the next chapter, you will learn the flip formula.

Chapter Eight: The Flip Formula

In real estate investing, a little math is involved. Don't worry, it's not that complicated, but you do want to know how much money you need to invest in each flip and how much profit you stand to make. These calculations need to be done on the front end to determine if the deal is right for you.

The first thing you need to know as a house flipper is the 70% rule. "The 70% rule says that an investor should spend no more than 70% of a property's after repair value (ARV) on a property. This includes the price you pay for the property itself, as well as any estimated repair costs" (Ball, 2020).

You want to start with determining your ARV. You can determine this by shopping the comps in the area. Multiply your ARV by 0.7 to determine your 70% figure. Next, you want to deduct your anticipated repair costs, which you would receive from your contractor from your 70% number.

For example, let's assume your ARV is $250,000.

Multiply 250,000 by .70, which equals $175,000.

You would talk to your contractor, and they will tell you that your repair costs will be $50,000. Subtract this number from your 70% number, which leaves you with $125,000. This is your maximum purchase price to turn a profit on this deal (How to flip houses...as simple as 5th grade math).

Chapter Summary

- Follow the 70% rule to make a profit

- Determine your ARV and follow the 70% formula to learn your max spending on a property.

In the next chapter, you will learn how to look at properties.

Chapter Nine: Looking at Properties

As you search for the perfect house to flip, there will be characteristics that you will want to consider beyond just the location. Physical characteristics play an important role in determining if your potential flip is viable.

The first thing you want to do is compare your potential flip with comparable homes in the area. Is it a 2-bedroom home when all the other houses in the neighborhood have three bedrooms? This is important to know because it will affect the overall market value of the home.

As you are observing physical characteristics of the house, look for areas that need work. This is an indication that it might be a good flip property. Does the lawn look overgrown and neglected? Does it look like it's been a while since someone has lived there?

Take the time to tour other homes in the area to see the pros and cons of your competition. Be creative when coming up with ways to leverage your flip, but make reasonable choices that don't step outside of the scope of the neighborhood; otherwise, you risk compromising your profit potential (How to choose a house to flip).

Chapter Summary

- Research your competition.

- Observe physical characteristics of the home.

- Be creative in your rehab solutions.

In the next chapter, you will learn how to make your first offer.

Chapter Ten: Making Offers

As you get ready to make your first offer on your flip, preparation is key. Know exactly what you want and what you are trying to accomplish. Establish your goals for the deal and be prepared to stick by those goals.

- It's okay to walk away. Although it may be easy to get attached to your first property, it is more important that you're attached to your budget. Be prepared to walk away if you are unable to negotiate the right numbers for your deal.

- Give the last concession in the negotiating process to maintain your posture. Whether it is closing costs or something else, you will likely go back and forth with the seller. Make sure you say the last word and offer the last concession.

- Distract your seller with a red herring tactic. Take the focus off the actual negotiating price and tilt it toward something else, like an item in the home that you'd like to convey.

- Penalize the seller for asking for multiple concessions. This is more of a training technique than anything else to let the seller know that you won't budge on your offer.

- Stand by your numbers. If you are working with an experienced negotiator, they will do their best to sway you from your set numbers. You walked in with a goal in mind. You know what you're trying to accomplish and exactly what you'll need to accomplish that goal. Don't falter.

- Don't get offended. You never know how a seller might react to your offer. Don't take anything personally. Keep it professional. If they want to remain in the deal, they will stay at the table. Keep your poker face on.

- Use data. Half of your job as an investor is analytics. Use those to your advantage at the negotiating table. Justify your actions through numbers (Turner, 13 tips for real estate negotiation).

Chapter Summary

- Be prepared at the negotiating table.

- Know what you want and stick to your numbers.

In the next chapter, you will learn about due diligence.

Chapter Eleven: Your Due Diligence

Before we dive into this chapter, let's first define due diligence. Due diligence is "investigation or audit of a potential or product to confirm all of the facts" (Syrios, The ultimate guide to due diligence). Research is imperative to successful real estate investment. Without proper due diligence, you risk sabotaging your deal. Don't skip this step. There's nothing fun or sexy about due diligence, but it's necessary.

Here are the areas you must consider in your due diligence efforts:

- **Area analysis.** You want to make sure the area you chose will yield you a profit. Research your area thoroughly. Do the math. Conduct your AMV to see what properties make sense and which ones don't. Know how much your rehab will cost. Lack of due diligence in this area would be extremely costly.

- **Physical inspections.** When looking at a home, make sure your due diligence is expansive. You might be looking at homes that need a lot of work, but make sure the amount of work needed doesn't exceed the anticipated budget.

- **Know your money.** Make sure your budget is reasonable based on the research you've already done. Run all the numbers to make sure everything makes sense and you stand to make a profit before going to the negotiating table.

- Never skip an inspection. Inspections will reveal things about the house that you can't see on the surface. You don't want to get stuck with a home that has structural issues and will cost you thousands of dollars because you neglected your due diligence on the inspection side (Syrios, The ultimate guide to due diligence).

Chapter Summary

- Don't skip due diligence, even though it may seem boring.

- Due diligence pre-offer.

- Due diligence post-offer.

In the next chapter, you will learn how to create your scope of work.

Chapter Twelve: Create Your SOW

Your SOW, or rehab scope of work, is the blueprint to properly managing your rehab. Building a scope of work is essential to maximizing your profit potential, accuracy, and efficiency while minimizing your risk.

When an investor builds their SOW, it should consist of six major parts.

1. **Build an overview and description.** This is your overall summary of the entire project. It will outline general information about the property and basic components of the rehab. At the end of your overview, you will outline the contractors needed to fulfill the tasks of this rehab project.

2. **Exterior.** This is going to cover all the work that needs to be completed on the outside of the home, such as the roof, windows, landscaping, and doors, just to name a few. Anything outside the home that needs to be updated should be included in this part of the report. If the rehab includes a new fence or deck, that should be included in this section.

3. **Interior.** This will include the inside perimeter of the home, such as walls, floors, molding, and light fixtures. If walls need to be knocked down to open up an area, this will be included in this section. If walls need to be painted, carpet installed, or hardwood floors refinished, this will be included here.

4. **Kitchen.** The kitchen is often one of the most expensive rooms in a home to renovate, which is why it gets its own section. New cabinets, countertops, appliances, and backsplashes will be included here.

5. **Bathrooms.** Bathrooms are big selling features in a home and will likely be included in your scope. This section of your report will include everything from the tub/shower, toilet, vanity, light fixtures, and paint.

6. **Plumbing and electrical.** This will include everything from the outlets, hot water heater, and light switches. If you opt to add a room to the house, like a bathroom, or you plan to move a laundry room, you will have to invest in the plumbing and electrical (Merrill, How to write a rehab scope of work).

As you are building your SOW, it is important to anticipate what your buyers will like. This is why your due diligence is so important. It will reveal what is trending in the market and what is attracting buyers and driving more sales. For example, many buyers love open concept. Consider this as you are building your SOW to make sure your home is accommodating this demand. You also want to utilize as much space as possible in the home. Buyers don't like to walk into a home and see wasted space. To them, this is wasted money. Make use of all the space you have. Be creative and show your buyers how to best utilize it. Keep everything neutral. Don't allow your personal taste to interfere with your profit potential. Vanilla is best if you want to attract the most potential buyers (Merrill, How to write a rehab scope of work).

Chapter Summary

- The SOW is the blueprint for managing your rehab.

- Build your SOW based on what your buyers might like.

In thenext chapter, you will learn how to create your rehab budget.

Chapter Thirteen: Create Your Budget

We have discussed the foundations for building your rehab budget. Your due diligence includes researching comps in the area and determining how your flip matches up against them. This will enable you to calculate your ARV and assist you in determining what a reasonable budget for your flip should be.

Once you've determined your ARV, conduct a walkthrough of your property with a contractor to assess the repairs that need to be made to reach your ARV and earn your maximum profit. The contractor will be able to assess what your total budget will be for the rehab. Don't forget to include a contingency in your budget to account for surprises. As soon as you begin the rehab process and start to open up walls, you're likely to run into repair issues that you did not account for. This is why a contingency is necessary. 10% is a reasonable amount of contingency to include in your budget. It's like an insurance policy—you may not use all of it, but you do want to be prepared (Correctly estimating your rehab budget).

Chapter Summary

- Conduct your due diligence and calculate your ARV.

- Walk through your property with a contractor to itemize your expenses.

In the next chapter, you will learn how to create your schedule.

Chapter Fifteen: Hiring Contractors

The contractors you choose for your flip can make or break your project. Choosing the wrong contractor can result in loss of profit, and in some cases, even forfeit the entire flip. We are not telling you this as a scare tactic; it is important that you take the process of hiring your contractors seriously. You need to take your time to ensure this process is done right because there are a lot of bad contractors out there that will steal your money, but the good thing is that there are a lot of good contractors too. Consider these suggestions as you interview your contractors, and you will be well on your way to a successful flip with a strong team you can use over and over again.

- **Always get references.** But, don't just stop at references from the contractor themselves. Of course they are going to refer you to people that make them look good. You need outside references beyond who they refer you to. Ideally, a reference from someone you know or trust works best, but before you hire the contractor, just make sure you get references from more sources than who they give you. As a rule of thumb, three to five references are acceptable.

- **Interview at least three contractors.** You want to interview and get quotes from at least three contractors. It doesn't matter if you feel a special connection with the first one you meet. Stick to the rule of three. You cannot make an informed decision with just one bid.

- **Compare each contractor.** Write down what you like about each contractor and what you don't like. Make sure they are apples to apples comparisons. One contractor might be more expensive but bring more to the table than the other two. How valuable is that to you? Keep a detailed list to help you make an informed decision once the process is over.

- **Make sure your contractors are licensed and insured.** This is self explanatory and will serve to protect you and your project. This should be non-negotiable.

- **Treat the process like a job interview.** If you don't like the way the contractor communicates, and they show up late for your first appointment, you probably don't want to work with them. Professionalism is necessary.

- **Know their payment terms.** Get their payment terms in writing at the outset of your relationship. Make sure it is clear what is expected on both sides. Do you pay half up front and half after the job is done? Whatever you agree to, make sure it is reasonable and to the benefit of you both (Naftulin, 2016).

Following these steps as you prepare to hire your contractors will not only serve you well on this flip, but for future flips too. It may require that you invest a bit of time upfront, but isn't it worth it if you can build your team of contractors now and not have to do it again? It's possible if you take the time to hire correctly.

Chapter Summary

- Your contractors will make or break your flip.

- Take your time hiring the right contractors, and you might never have to do it again.

- Interview your contractors like they're on a job interview.

In the next chapter, you will learn how to manage your rehab.

Chapter Sixteen: Managing Your Rehab

If you follow all the steps outlined in this book, you should have no problem managing your rehab. Having a strong scope of work and a schedule to follow will ensure that you have a blueprint to follow throughout the process. Stick to this blueprint. That doesn't mean you cannot allow room for flexibility, but the further you veer away from your timeline, the more it will eat into your overall profit. The best way to make sure you stay on track with your schedule is to have strong contractors. We reviewed in the last chapter the importance of hiring great contractors and the impact they can have on your project. Good contractors are good for their word, and you can trust them to complete their tasks when they say they will. Bad contractors can stretch a project for days and even weeks. If you see signs of this creeping in with one of your contractors, don't hesitate to fire them. Firing a contractor does mean that you will have to invest time in finding a replacement, but how much more time and money will be lost if you continue to work with them on projects with never-ending deadlines? Don't be afraid to let a contractor go if things are not going the way they should. You will lose time in the project as a result of their performance, but not as much time as you will lose if you choose to keep them on the project.

Hiring a general contractor can help you stay on top of the project as the general contractor will be responsible for being on site everyday and overseeing every aspect of the project. Many general contractors come with their own crews because they've had experience on projects and know who works best at each task. However, like any other contractor, make sure you interview and vet them as well. You want to make sure you can trust someone you're giving that much authority to. Also, whether you have a general contractor on board or not, don't make the mistake of thinking you don't need to show up at the work site daily too. This is your project and your investment. Make sure you're present and aware of everything that is happening on your work site. You have a vested interest in everything that is going on there. One of the biggest mistakes novice flippers make is not showing up at the work site.

Chapter Summary

- Stick to your scope of work, your blueprint.

- Don't be afraid to fire a contractor if they are not performing.

- Consider hiring a general contractor.

- Show up at the worksite.

In the next chapter, you will learn whether to use an agent or for sale by owner.

Chapter Seventeen: Agent or FSBO?

We talked about the value of partnering with an agent earlier in this book, but what about for sale by owner, or FSBO? As an investor, do you have to choose? Not necessarily. There is value in utilizing both to secure good real estate deals.

First, when you are partnering with an agent, like all of your partnerships, you want to make sure they are carefully vetted. A real estate agent can be your greatest ally if chosen correctly. When searching for an agent, you are looking for someone who can do much more than just show homes. An agent needs to be:

- **A strong negotiator.** You want to work with an agent that can help you secure deals and get them at a great price. As an investor, you are looking for deals under market value, and to achieve this, you must be a master negotiator.

- **Highly responsive.** Your agent needs to be available and able to respond at a moment's notice.

- **They know the local market.** You want to work with an agent that knows the market well. They are well-researched and up to speed on everything about your local neighborhoods.

- **They know investing.** You want to work with a real estate agent who has experience working with investors. They know and understand your world and leverage themselves as an asset.

- **Network.** You want to work with an agent who is well-networked. They know other mortgage brokers and people in the industry who all have their fingers on the pulse of what is happening in the real estate market (Yale, 2019).

For sale by owner (FSBO) is more of a grassroots approach to real estate investing. You will likely run into more FSBO opportunities when you drive for dollars. One of the biggest benefits of FSBO is that you are often dealing directly with the owner and don't have to pay out a commission to an agent on the sale. The con is that you will have to do everything that a realtor would normally do, like negotiating. As a new investor, this may be a skill you have yet to develop, so it might be to your advantage to work with a realtor rather than focus on FSBO opportunities. As you build more experience as an investor and have a few deals behind you, FSBO might be a great strategy to consider.

Chapter Summary

- Agents are great allies, but take the time to properly vet them before working with them.

- Agents should be master negotiators and have experience working with investors.

- FSBO is a great grassroots opportunity, but not ideal for new investors.

In the next chapter, you will learn the importance of staging.

Chapter Eighteen: Staging

This is a step in the process that is easy for new investors to skip, simply because they don't want to spend the money. Put yourself in the buyer's shoes. How much more likely are you to buy a home that is staged versus one that is not? Have you ever visited a model home in a new construction community? The model homes always have a rich, homely feel because they want the buyers to experience what the home would feel like if it was theirs. Now let's take a look at some numbers in case you're still not convinced.

- 58% of seller's realtors said their homes sold for more money because their homes were staged.

- In a survey of 3,500 staged homes, 46% sold for 10% more.

- Homes staged pre-listed averaged less than 30 days on the market (Cohen, 2019).

The bottom line is that staging puts money back in your pocket as an investor. You could choose to DIY staging or hire a professional. As a new investor, hiring a professional is recommended because you are new to this process, and you want it done right. It is an expense to hire a professional stager, but you see the statistics on staging; it's an investment that is worth it.

Chapter Summary

- Staging is an investment that puts money back into your pocket.

- Consider hiring a professional stager for the best results.

In the next chapter, you will learn about buyer due diligence.

Chapter Nineteen: Buyer Due Diligence

Just as you conducted your due diligence when you purchased your property, you can expect your buyer to do the same. Some will be more diligent than others. Regardless, you need to be prepared to address their due diligence. If you've done your due diligence, you should have no problem matching theirs. Make sure you know what your property is worth and be prepared to stand firm on your offer. If you've prepared as you should, you will allow a degree of flexibility at the negotiating table, but it is essential that you keep your poker face and know your limit.

If your buyer has done their due diligence, they will ask for an inspection. This should not be a cause for concern if you have done your due diligence and ordered an inspection when you purchased the property and addressed any issues that came up. If, however, you left any of those issues outstanding, you must be prepared to offer concessions to your buyer once their inspection report comes back. That is the right and ethical thing to do.

The same is true of the appraisal. Proper due diligence on your part will ensure that you don't run into any problems here. If you don't get your house appraised prior to the sale, you risk losing profit if it doesn't appraise at your asking price. The bank will not finance above the appraisal, so make sure you have prepared in advance for this. Make sure your home will meet these requirements so it doesn't tie up your deal.

It is also possible that your buyer's financing can fall through due to last minute credit issues, job changes, or debt to income. Make sure your buyer is fully approved before you get to the closing table to avoid the risk of financing falling through. This is a common issue when buyers are pre-qualified with their lender instead of receiving approval (What to do after having a mortgage loan denied at closing, 2019).

Chapter Summary

- Buyers will conduct due diligence during their process, just like you.

- Conducting your due diligence will ensure you don't run into any issues during their due diligence.

- Be prepared for inspections and appraisals, and make sure you've done your homework for financing and that it's not held up.

- Make sure your buyer's financing is solid.

In the next chapter, you will learn about the closing.

Chapter Twenty: The Closing

The closing is the last part of your real estate deal. Once you reach the closing table, you are in the home stretch and one step closer to earning your first profit on a real estate deal. However, snags can come up at the closing table. That is why due diligence is so important. It helps to avoid any potential problems when you get this far down the road. There are several steps involved in the closing process. For your closing to be successful, none of these should be skipped.

- **Title insurance.** You will need to hire a title company to conduct a title search. More formally, "a title search is an examination of public records to determine and confirm a property's legal ownership and find out what claims, if any, exist on the property" (Seth, 2021).

- **Hire an attorney.** It is not required that you have an attorney present at the closing table, but it is highly recommended. A real estate attorney is going to be well-versed in the jargon and speech at the closing table. As a novice investor, it is important that you build strong allies with professionals that have more experience in this area than you do. Bring an attorney to the closing table.

- **Negotiate closing costs.** We have already covered negotiation earlier in this book. It is highly likely that your buyer will seek to have you cover closing costs in this deal. If you have done adequate preparation, you will know what you plan to cover, what you will not, and why. Stick to your plan.

- **Remove contingencies.** When you are sitting at the closing table, it's time to put a bow on the deal, and thus time to remove any contingencies that might exist with it. When you remove these contingencies, it must be stated in writing when these requests will be satisfied. For example, if you have repairs in a contingency, you must state when that repair will be completed.

- **Be prepared to sign a lot of paperwork.** If you've ever bought a home before, you know it comes with a lot of paperwork. This is no different; you are just on the seller side instead of the buyer side (Seth, 2021).

All money will be placed in escrow during the closing process to protect the interests of both the buyer and the seller. Once the closing process is complete, that money will be released from escrow. That is when you, our new investor friend, will get paid.

Chapter Summary

- The closing is the home stretch, but it is possible to run into snags.

- Follow the closing process to preserve your deal and profits.

Final Words

The world of house flipping and real estate investing is highly lucrative, but it is not something you should enter lightly. Contrary to what many people think, it is hard work and requires a significant investment of time and energy. Can you earn significant money as a house flipper? Absolutely! How much you earn will depend how much time and energy you want to put into it. As you can see, there are a lot of considerations when you are flipping a house. It's not a one-step process. It requires a lot of research. As a matter of fact, research is something you will spend a lot of your time doing. Without proper due diligence and knowledge of your market, you will end up making bad deals and even worse choices. The fact that you're reading this book is a good sign because this is step one of your due diligence. If you take the time to follow the steps in this book to acquire your first property, you've shown real commitment to the process.

It is advised that you don't skip any of the steps outlined in this book—not if you want to be a successful flipper. I understand if you thought you wouldn't have to manage anyone when you made the choice to become a real estate investor. But the reality is, yes, you will have to manage a team, that is, unless you plan to do all the work yourself, and we all know that is not the case. You will need to manage your team of contractors and it is important that you stay on them to manage your deadline. One way to combat this issue is to hire a general contractor. As we mentioned before, hiring a general contractor doesn't negate your responsibility as the investor. You still need to be onsite for the rehab. If you are still working during your flip, you are probably concerned about whether or not you can be present on site each day. That's where having a general contractor on site is even more valuable. You can have someone there serving as your eyes and ears when you can't be. But, even if you happen to have a demanding job that is keeping you from being on the site daily, make a point of being there at least a couple times a week. This is your flip, which means you should be invested in making sure that every aspect of the project goes as planned.

As a novice flipper, one of the most valuable things you can do is build allies and partnerships. We talked about networking and working with real estate agents earlier in this book. Early in your real estate career, this is extremely important because you want to glean from their expertise. As a new flipper, you are anxious to get involved with deals like distressed properties and foreclosures. But, we advise that you take your time in deals like this because their success hinges on experience. Build your network of partners and advisors and that will accelerate your growth as a new investor. The more you humble yourself and learn from their experience, the quicker you will move from a novice to an experienced investor. Plus, you will learn the value of a team around you as you grow in the business. Remember that old acronym for team—together, everyone accomplishes more. It's true.

Lastly, we advise that you take the time to build documents, like your scope of work. We understand that it's not fun and probably will feel like you're writing a report, but look at it as your blueprint to your flip. Think of it as a money document because that is exactly what it is. In real estate investing, the more prepared you are, the better. Building your scope of work forces you to think about the project and your anticipated outcomes. It lays out your plan and what you envision for the project. When you can start to build a vision for your project, it ignites your excitement for the project because then, you can learn more about what it can be. The most important thing to realize throughout this process is that it is not about you and your personal preferences. Part of your research is learning what the market wants and answering those needs. That is why we suggested that you tour the comps in your neighborhood to get a sense of what is trending and what the homes look like. You should build your finishes in your flip based on the information you learn from this process.

Not to beat a dead horse here, but like we said earlier, don't skip any steps. If you take the time to follow each step outlined in this book carefully, you will be well on your way to being a successful flipper. Take your time easing into the process. This is not an overnight process, but if you are steady and diligent, you will build a strong income as a real estate investor. Like we said earlier, don't try to do it all on your own. There is power in your team, and you want to leverage it to close as many deals as possible.

We are excited for you to accomplish your goals as a new real estate flipper. Now get out there and make some money!

If you enjoyed this book in anyway, an honest review is always appreciated!